ROCK EXPLORER

This book should be returned to any branch of the
Lancashire County Library on or before the date shown

20 MAR 2019
18 SEP 2019
28 FEB 2020
28 JUL 2021

Lancashire County Library,
County Hall Complex,
1st floor Christ Church Precinct,
Preston, PR1 8XJ
www.lancashire.gov.uk/libraries

Lancashire County Council

LL1(A)

CKS

Claudia Martin

D1335678

QED
LANCASHIRE COUNTY LIBRARY
30118136800186

Quarto is the authority on a wide range of topics.

Quarto educates, entertains and enriches the lives of our readers—enthusiasts and lovers of hands-on living.

www.quartoknows.com

Editor: Clare Hibbert
Designer: Dave Ball

© 2018 Quarto Publishing plc
Text © Claudia Martin

First Published in 2017 by QED Publishing,
an imprint of The Quarto Group.
The Old Brewery, 6 Blundell Street,
London N7 9BH, United Kingdom.
T (0)20 7700 6700 F (0)20 7700 8066
www.QuartoKnows.com

All rights reserved. No part of this publication may be reproduced, stored in a retrieval system, or transmitted in any form or by any means, electronic, mechanical, photocopying, recording, or otherwise, without the prior permission of the publisher, nor be otherwise circulated in any form of binding or cover other than that in which it is published and without a similar condition being imposed on the subsequent purchaser.

A catalogue record for this book is available from the British Library.

ISBN 978-1-78493-965-6

Manufactured in Guangdong, China TT022018

9 8 7 6 5 4 3 2 1

FSC www.fsc.org MIX Paper from responsible sources FSC® C016973

Lancashire Library Services

30118136800186	
PETERS	J552MAR
£6.99	18-May-2018
NPO	

Contents

What is a Rock? 4
Igneous Rock 6
Sedimentary Rock 8
Metamorphic Rock 10
Amazing Patterns 12
Strange Shapes 14
Deep Caves 16
Useful Rock 18
Rock Art 20
Rock Guide 22
Glossary 23
Index 24

What is **a Rock?**

There are hundreds of types of rock. Some are hard, some are crumbly – and some are very strange!

This tower is made of a rock called sandstone. It is in Arizona, USA.

ROCKY PLANET

Rock covers our planet. In some places bare rock is visible, but rock also lies under cities, soil and oceans.

Rock families

There are three kinds of rock: igneous, sedimentary and metamorphic. Each kind forms in a different way.

Igneous **Sedimentary** **Metamorphic**

Granite is an igneous rock that contains different coloured minerals.

MINERAL MIXTURES

Rocks are mixtures of different minerals. Minerals grow in the ground or in water. They are solids.

Igneous **Rock**

Deep inside the Earth is hot, runny rock called magma. When magma cools, it hardens to form igneous rock.

ERUPTION!
Some igneous rocks form when magma bursts onto the Earth's surface.

When magma erupts from a volcano it is called lava.

Obsidian forms when magma erupts from a volcano, then cools very fast.

Pumice forms when bubbly magma is thrown from a volcano.

Underground activity

Not all igneous rocks form at the surface. Gabbro is created when magma cools underground.

Gabbro

The Giant's Causeway is made of slabs of basalt. The basalt formed when runny magma cooled and cracked.

ROUTE ACROSS THE SEA

According to legend, a giant built the Giant's Causeway in Northern Ireland. He needed to cross the sea to fight a Scottish giant.

Sedimentary **Rock**

Sedimentary rocks are made when pebbles, minerals or dead animals and plants are pressed together.

Chalk is a soft, crumbly rock.

WHITE CLIFFS

Chalk is made from seashells that collected on the seabed. After millions of years, they hardened into rock.

LAYER ON LAYER

Look for layers of different materials in sedimentary rocks. Sandstone is pressed sand. Mudstone and shale are pressed mud.

These stripes are layers of sandstone and mudstone.

ON THE MOVE

Earth is covered by massive, slow-moving plates of rock. They push land together or pull it apart. What was once seabed can end up far inland.

These pointed pieces of limestone formed from shells and corals. The area is now a desert!

Metamorphic **Rock**

Any rock can change into metamorphic rock. All it takes is great heat or pressure.

MOVING PLATES

Rock sometimes comes under pressure from the movement of Earth's plates. This can squash or fold the rock.

This metamorphic rock, schist, has been bent and folded.

Slate is shale that has been pressed. Shale is a sedimentary rock made from mud.

HEATING UP

Many metamorphic rocks are made when rocks get very hot. This can happen deep inside the Earth.

The metamorphic rock marble is limestone that has been heated. Its swirling colours are made by minerals in the limestone.

Precious gems

Some metamorphic rocks contain secrets. Precious gems can grow from minerals trapped in the super-hot rock.

This ruby formed inside a slab of marble.

Amazing **Patterns**

Some rocks are striped or lumpy. The patterns tell us how the rocks were made.

BRILLIANT BANDS
Stripes can form in metamorphic rocks. It happens when pressing, sliding or heat separate the different minerals in the rock.

Gneiss has stripes of dark and light minerals.

UNUSUAL SURFACES

Sedimentary rocks often form with lumps and bumps.

Mineral grains called ooliths settled on this limestone.

Conglomerate is mudstone or sandstone with pebbles trapped in it.

ANCIENT LIFE FORMS

Some sedimentary rocks are patterned with fossils.

Ferns were preserved in this sandstone.

Rainbow mountains

The striped mountains in Danxia, China, are made of different-coloured sandstones. The layers were pushed and turned by the Earth's plates.

Strange **Shapes**

Wind, rain and rivers can rub rocks into weird shapes. This is called erosion.

AMAZING ARCHES

Arches can form when wind and water wear away soft rock. Harder rock is left behind.

Carved canyon

The Grand Canyon in Arizona, USA, is 446 km long. It was worn away by the Colorado River.

STUNNING STACKS

Waves and wind can wear cliffs into towers called stacks. The Twelve Apostles are limestone stacks off the coast of Australia.

Only eight of the Twelve Apostles are left.

FAIRY CHIMNEYS

Odd pillars of rock are sometimes called fairy chimneys or hoodoos.

A sandstone arch in Utah, USA

Fairy chimneys in central Turkey

Hoodoos in Utah, USA

Deep **Caves**

Deep, dark caves can be found underground. They are worn away by water.

DISSOLVING ROCK

When rainwater or water from an underground river soaks into limestone, the rock dissolves. Tiny grains of rock mix with the water and are carried away.

These limestone caves are in Slovenia.

Slow growers

Even the fastest stalactites form quite slowly – just 3 mm per year!

Some minerals dangle from the ceiling as stalactites.

DRIP, DRIP

Water containing the dissolved minerals drips into the cave. It leaves some minerals behind.

Some minerals collect below a dripping stalactite. They build up into towers called stalagmites.

Useful **Rock**

Humans have used rocks for thousands of years. There are useful rocks everywhere!

STONE AGE

Before people knew how to work with metal, they used hard rocks to make weapons and tools.

BUILDING BLOCKS

Strong, sturdy rock can create beautiful buildings.

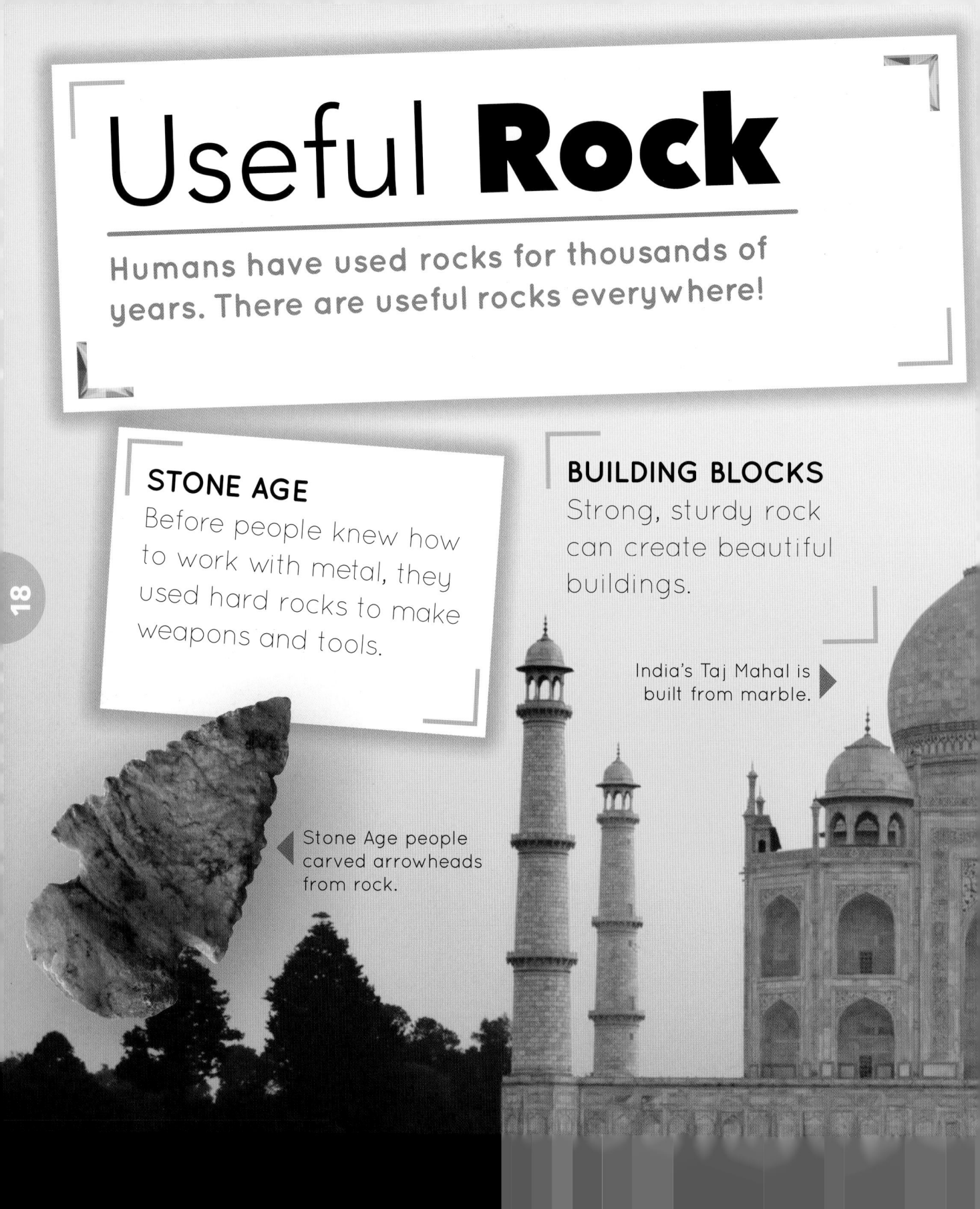

Stone Age people carved arrowheads from rock.

India's Taj Mahal is built from marble.

FOSSIL FUEL

Coal is a sedimentary rock made of plants that died millions of years ago.

▲ Coal is burnt as a fuel.

▲ Gravel helps water to drain away.

GREAT GRAVEL

Pieces of rock, called gravel, are used to build roads.

Deepest mine

Miners dig into rocks to find useful minerals, such as gold and salt. The deepest mines go several kilometres into the ground.

Rock **Art**

Rocks can be turned into amazing art. They can be carved, moulded or painted.

SUPER SAND

Sand is found on beaches and in deserts, where waves or wind break rock into little pieces.

Buddhist monks used coloured sand to make this mandala.

STONE CARVING

It takes years of practice to carve stone into statues or furniture.

This sculptor is using a chisel to carve stone.

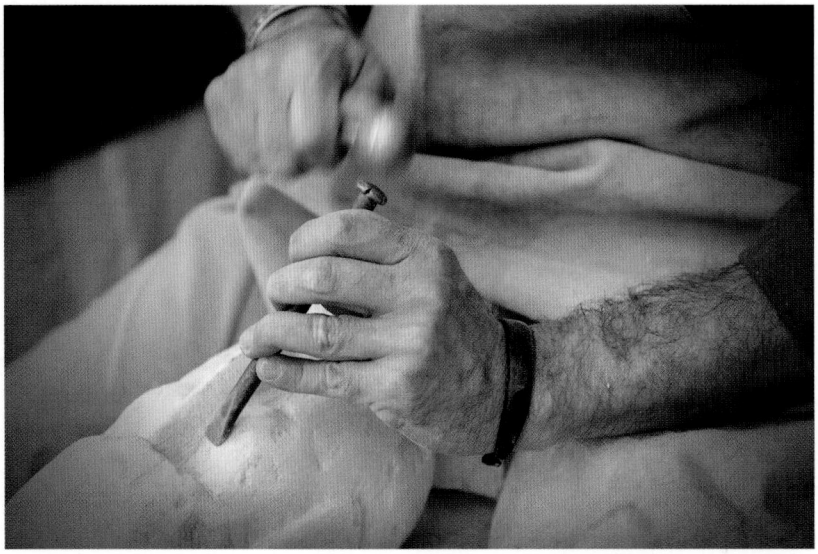

Cave paintings

Around 40,000 years ago, humans started to paint the walls of caves. They often drew the animals they hunted.

Lascaux Cave, France

PERFECT POTS

Clay is a soft rock. It was formed from plants and minerals mixed with water.

After clay is shaped, it can be hardened by heating it.

Rock **Guide**

BASALT
Type: Igneous
Description: Dark grey and hard

CHALK
Type: Sedimentary
Description: White, soft and crumbly

CLAY
Type: Sedimentary
Description: White to brownish-orange; soft when wet

COAL
Type: Sedimentary
Description: Brown or black; easy to burn

CONGLOMERATE
Type: Sedimentary
Description: Rounded pebbles cemented into sandstone or mudstone

GRANITE
Type: Igneous
Description: Grey or pinkish with grains of coloured minerals

LIMESTONE
Type: Sedimentary
Description: Grey to yellowish; slowly dissolves in rainwater

MARBLE
Type: Metamorphic
Description: White or pink to blue, green or black; can have swirling patterns

OBSIDIAN
Type: Igneous
Description: Dark, very hard and shiny

PUMICE
Type: Igneous
Description: Pale, full of holes and lightweight

SANDSTONE
Type: Sedimentary
Description: Sand-coloured, from white to black; rough and grainy

SLATE
Type: Metamorphic
Description: Usually grey; easy to split into flat sheets

Glossary

dissolves Mixes in with water or another liquid.

erosion Wearing away by wind, water or ice.

fossil The remains of an animal or plant that lived long ago, pressed into rock or turned into rock.

fuel A material that is burnt to make heat.

gemstone A beautiful and hard mineral or rock that is used in jewellery.

igneous rock Rock formed when magma cools down and hardens.

magma Hot, runny rock that lies beneath Earth's surface of cool, hardened rock.

mandala A round picture that represents the universe for Hindus or Buddhists.

metamorphic rock Rock formed when any type of rock is changed by heat or pressure.

mineral A solid formed in the ground or in water.

plate One of the giant slabs of rock that make up the surface of the Earth.

pressure A pressing force.

rock A solid made from different minerals.

sedimentary rock Rock formed when sand, mud, minerals or plant and animal remains are pressed together until they harden.

Index

arches **14–15**
arts **20–21**

basalt **7, 22**
buildings **18–19**

carving **18, 20, 21**
caves **16–17, 21**
chalk **8, 22**
cities **4**
clay **21, 22**
coal **19, 22**
conglomerate **13, 22**

erosion **14–15, 16, 23**

fairy chimneys **15**
ferns **13**

gabbro **7**
gemstones **11, 23**
Giant's Causeway **7**
gneiss **12**
gold **19**
Grand Canyon **14**
granite **5, 22**
gravel **19**

hoodoos **15**

igneous rock **5, 6–7, 22, 23**

Lascaux Cave **21**
limestone **9, 11, 13, 15, 16, 22**

magma **6, 7, 23**
mandalas **20, 23**
marble **11, 18, 22**
metamorphic rock **5, 10–11, 12, 22, 23**
minerals **5, 8, 11, 12, 13, 17, 19, 21, 22, 23**
mining **19**
mudstone **9, 13, 22**

obsidian **7, 22**
oceans **4**
ooliths **13**

paintings **20, 21**
pebbles **13, 22**
plates **9, 10, 13, 23**
pressure **10, 23**
pumice **7, 22**

rubies **11**

salt **19**
sand **9, 20, 23**
sandstone **4–5, 9, 13, 14–15, 22**
schist **10**
seabed **8, 9**
sedimentary rock **5, 8–9, 11, 13, 19, 22, 23**
shale **9, 11**
slate **11, 22**
soil **4**
stacks **15**
stalactites **17**
stalagmites **17**
Stone Age **18**

Taj Mahal **18–19**
Twelve Apostles **15**

volcanoes **6, 7**

water **5, 14, 16, 17, 21, 23**

PICTURE CREDITS

Alamy: 10b (Sabena Jane Blackbird), 16 (Michael Runkel/robertharding), 17t (Michael Runkel/robertharding), 17b (Frans Lanting Studio); **Dreamstime:** 11br (Farbled); **Shutterstock:** cover (www.sandatlas.org, Tyler Boyes, vvoe, urbazon), 1 (Valentina Razumova), 2–3 (Brian S.), 3tr (Reamolko), 4–5 (Zbynek Plinta), 5tl (kavring), 5ctl (Fokin Oleg), 5ctr (vvoe), 5tr (vvoe), 6 (Ammit Jack), 7tl (paleontologist natural), 7c (vvoe), 7tr (vvoe), 7b (S-F), 8 (Peter Cripps), 9t (pongsakom matapan), 9b (David Steele), 11t (Paul J. Martin), 11bc (cheyennezj), 12–13t (Sementer), 12–13b (ruiztome), 12bl (www.sandatlas.org), 13r (Sementer), 13br (dinozzaver), 14–15 (TRphotos), 14b (Josemaria Toscano), 15tr (Greg Brave), 15cb (Matyas Rehak), 15br (ronnybas), 17tr (Gurcharan Singh), 18–19 (Luciano Mortula/LGM), 18bl (I. Pilon), 19tl (maziarz), 19tr (bogdan ionescu), 19br (Mark Agnor), 20 (Tomo Jesenicnik), 21tl (davidsansegundo), 21tr (thipjang), 21b (kuzina), 22tlt (Tyler Boyes), 22tlb (Tyler Boyes), 22clt (fotosaga), 22clb (ffolas), 22blt (Fokin Oleg), 22blb (ballykdy), 22trt (Dr. Ajay Kumar Singh), 22trb (vvoe), 22crt (vvoe), 22crb (Vladislav S), 22brt (Aleksandr Pobedimskiy), 22brb (Tyler Boyes).